What is... ? See-through

Heinemann

First published in Great Britain by Heinemann Library
an imprint of Heinemann Publishers (Oxford) Ltd
Halley Court, Jordan Hill, Oxford OX2 8EJ

MADRID ATHENS PARIS
FLORENCE PRAGUE WARSAW
PORTSMOUTH NH CHICAGO SAO PAULO
SINGAPORE TOKYO MELBOURNE AUCKLAND
IBADAN GABORONE JOHANNESBURG

© Heinemann Publishers (Oxford) Ltd

Designed by Heinemann Publishers (Oxford) Ltd
Printed in China

99
10 9 8 7 6 5 4 3 2

ISBN 0431 07980 3

British Library Cataloguing in Publication Data
Warbrick, Sarah
See-through. - (What is...? Series)
I. Series
500

Acknowledgements
The Publishers would like to thank the following
for the kind loan of equipment and materials
used in this book: Spoils, Bishop Stortford.
Toys supplied by Toys Я Us Ltd,
the world's biggest toy megastore.

Special thanks to George, Jodie, Nadia and
Rose who appear in the photographs

Photographs: Network p15; OSF (Oxford Scientific Films) pp6-7;
Science Photo Library p19; other photographs by Trevor Clifford
Commissioned photography arranged by Hilary Fletcher
Cover Photography: Trevor Clifford

There are see-through things all around us.
See-through things let the light through.
See-through things show you what's inside.

This book shows you what is see-through.

These things look different.
What differences can you see?

In one way they are all the same.
They are all see-through.

Rose can see through a window.

That's because it is see-through.

The fish tank is see-through.

You can see all the pretty coloured fish.

You can see through this glass.

But doesn't Nadia look funny!

What do you think is inside
this paper bag?

You can see the apples when they
are inside a clear plastic bag.

These plastic containers are used
for storing things.

And you can still see what's inside.

You can see through these
swimming goggles.

They'll protect your eyes, too.

Water is see-through.

But it can still make things
look very different.

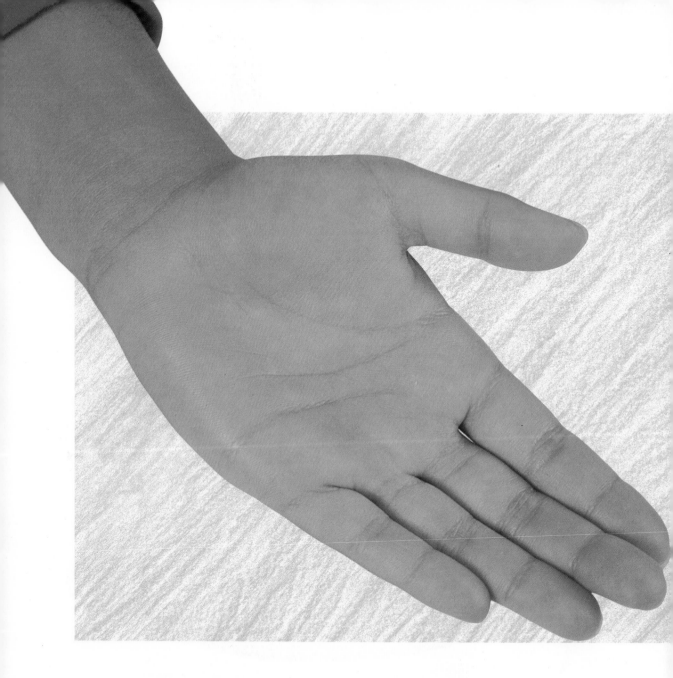

Your hand isn't see-through.

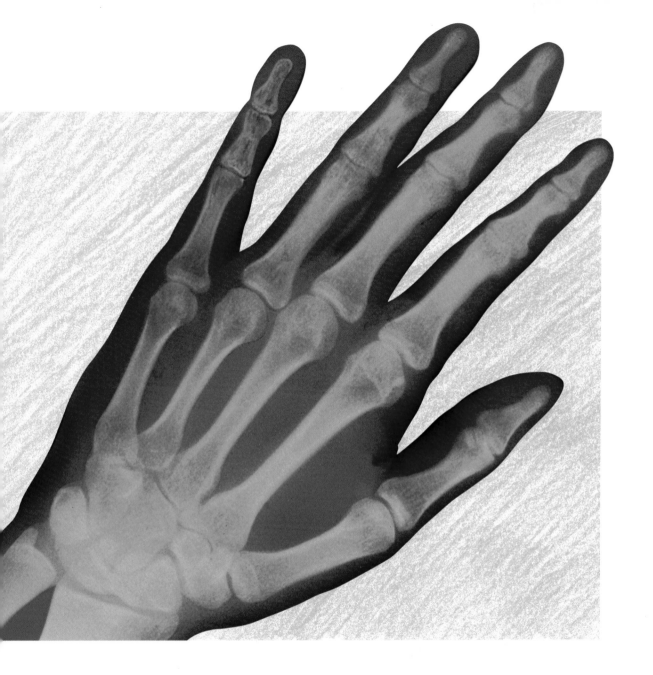

An X-ray picture can show you what's inside.

What is see-through here?

Index